DO2

(Celebrating His Faithfulness)

Volume 1

By

Eturuvie Erebor

Angela Steele

Annmarie Givans

Karen White

Kim Donaby

Julie Clark

Marilyn Smith

DOZ Devotional is published by Eturuvie Erebor in London, England

© Eturuvie Erebor 2016

All Rights Reserved

Dedication

This devotional is dedicated to Almighty God who gave the vision, and those He brought alongside me to fulfil it.

Eturuvie Erebor

Acknowledgement

My sincere appreciation goes to God who has blessed me in all ways. I celebrate His faithfulness in my life. And I am grateful to all who were part of the process of writing and publishing this book.

Eturuvie Erebor

Table of Contents

Day 1

Daughter of the King

(Part One of the *Identifying with Jesus' Love Series*)

Some of my earliest memories are pleasant. Some are not so pleasant. I had an overall feeling that I was somehow in the way or not worthy of attention. As a young girl, I felt worthless. As I grew into womanhood, I believed lies about God and myself. Anxiety weighed my heart, and uneasiness edged into my mind. Fear cast consuming lies, which attempted to coil me and choke life. Some lies included: "I'm not qualified, and I've no idea what I am doing. I sounded stupid. People are better off if I didn't help. I can't think on my own. I have to make everyone happy. I'd better make everyone else's issues the priority, even at my own detriment. No one cares. I'm abandoned." These thoughts continued for most of my life. I believed lies, bowing to them and accepting them as my identity. Although this low-grade anxiety still tries to grip me, I am on the other side of it.

It's as if, with righteous indignation, I've drawn a line in the sand, and although I can see from afar the lies that once crossed my boundary, they cannot touch me, because of Jesus. Recently, in the last few years, Jesus' true love flooded my heart. I know better now. My focus shifted. Rather than being self-focused, I have become Jesus-focused. Rather than identifying with lies, I am identifying with Jesus' love.

The Bible and the Holy Spirit remind me that God's acceptance isn't based on my performance. It's based on what Christ already promised, provided, and accomplished on the Cross. Even as I write these words, I shake my head in awe and wonder at the simplicity of the Gospel of Good News, which is the story of the Cross of Christ and His Resurrection. My faulty foundation led me to think God's love fluctuated with my performance. I viewed God as a rule keeper, as if He were more concerned about a list of rules and regulations, rather than a relationship. Fortunately, I realized my performance didn't dictate His pursuit of my heart. More than anything, He pursues my heart. He wants connection, and true relationship connects. In this divine relationship, Jesus opened my eyes to believe His Truth.

Meditate on this: *"Long before He laid down earth's foundations, He had us in mind, had settled on us as the focus of His love, to be made whole and holy by His love." Ephesians 1:4 MSG*

"Then Christ will make His home in your hearts as you trust in Him. Your roots will grow down into God's love and keep

you strong. And may you have the power to understand, as all God's people should, how wide, how long, how high, and how deep His love is." Ephesians 3:17, 18

Prayer: Father, what do you say about me? What you say about me is the truest thing about me. Who Christ is in me is the truest thing about me. Help me to see myself the way You see me, through Your eyes of love and acceptance. Help me to see others the way You see them, through Your eyes of love and acceptance. Jesus, I rest in Your love this day, as I turn my focus toward Your kindness and goodness. Thank You for Your love. In Jesus Name I pray, Amen.

Angela Steele

DAY 2

Jesus Pursues Us

(Part Two in the *Identifying with Jesus' Love Series*)

The truth is that Jesus initiates love, and His life-giving words soak my thirsty heart. Jesus approves of me, and He wants me. Jesus gives healing for hurt, grace for grief. He is attentive. "Everything about your life hinges on the answer to one simple question: Do you know how loved you really are?" writes Wayne Jacobson from his book entitled *He Loves Me! Learning to Live in the Father's Affection.* The Holy Spirit beckons us to rest. Hope heals the emotionally abandoned, the physically aching. Dismissed, discarded, and misunderstood hearts writhe from loneliness, but He comforts the broken hearted. Hollow hearts echo emptiness, but He fills them.

Once I began to understand how much Jesus really does love me, it dawned on me that I have options. A veil lifted from my eyes, and clouded thoughts became clear. My options are that I can believe and respond to a lie, or I can believe and respond to God's truth. Satan's scheme would have me adhering to lies that rendered me powerless. The truth is that

I already have power because of Jesus' finished work on the Cross. Here are a couple examples.

- Lie: "God won't help me. I'm unworthy. I messed up. I have nothing to offer."

- *Truth: God helps me. I am worthy. I have the mind of Christ. I have a lot to offer."*

- Lie: I am stuck in this mess.

- *Truth: All things are possible in Christ.*

As my mind started to be renewed to God's truth, new thought patterns dominated my thinking and decision-making. The circumstances and people hasn't changed, but my response to them has and continues to do so. I've started to ask the Father what He says, and new options thrill me.

I continually ask Jesus to help me see life through His eyes and to come into agreement with how much He loves me, how He sees me, and the tender truths He sings over me. How we perceive God colors how we see others and ourselves. Am I going to believe Satan's lies or my Savior's love? "Rejecting Satan's lie and accepting God's evaluation of us leads to a renewed hope, joy, and purpose in life," shares Robert S. McGee in his book called *The Search for Significance.* Who I am in Christ is the truest thing about me. He sees me as holy and pure. Renewing my mind to this fact is an ongoing adventure. "The Holy Spirit began to show me who I am in Jesus and told me that if I would just surrender my own opinion of myself and agree with His opinion of me, my heart would be made whole, and my life would be transformed," testifies Connie Witter in her book entitled *Living Loved Living Free- Experience the Freedom of Living in the Father's Love through the Finished Work of Jesus*. It's not all about us, and what we can accomplish. It's about Him, and what He has already accomplished. If you are apprehensive to believe what He says about you, simply ask Him to help you see yourself the way He sees you. Relief and rest are found in Him as we identify with who Jesus is and who He is in us.

Meditate on this: *"Are you tired? Worn out? Burned out on religion? Come to Me. Get away with Me and you'll recover your life. I'll show you how to take a real rest. Walk with Me and work with Me—watch how I do it. Learn the unforced rhythms of grace. I won't lay anything heavy or ill-fitting on you. Keep company with Me and you'll learn to live freely and lightly." Matthew 11:28-30 MSG*

Prayer: Jesus, thank You for pursuing me with Your gentle, tender love. I receive Your love. Help me this day to draw near to You. In Jesus Name I pray, Amen.

Angela Steele

DAY 3

Jesus' Righteousness is in Us

(Part Three in the *Identifying with Jesus' Love Series*)

As a Christian, *what* do I identify with on a daily basis? Do I identify with the crucified sin nature or Christ's nature in me? Am I a fearful slave or am I a daughter of the King? Am I a beggar of bread or the Bride of Christ? What is true of me at my core? Core is defined as the central or most important part of something. Is what I feel and my feelings about myself at my core true? Only what Jesus says about me at my core is true. Who Jesus is in me is the truest thing about me. If I see and identify myself contrary to how God sees and identifies me, then I am believing a lie at my core. My core, my heart determines the direction of my life. The only way to break free from a cycle of sin is to believe at my core that Jesus already made me righteous, based on His works, not mine.

Webster defines righteousness as "the state of being right with God; justification; the work of Christ." Because of the Blood of Jesus, there has been a complete change at the core of who I am. Daily, I ask the Holy Spirit to help me see myself and identify with who God has already made me to be in Him. I am not attaining to or striving for righteousness or to be righteous. As believers, we are already righteous. The Holy Spirit will produce that fruit in my life as I trust and rely on Him to help me see myself through God's eyes of love and acceptance. The Holy Spirit will bring about those heart changes as I turn to Jesus and rely and trust Him to change me from the inside.

Since Jesus is my Savior, there has been a change at the core of who I am. It's whether I recognize it and see it. Only the Holy Spirit made the Light go on for me. Only the Holy Spirit can give revelation. We enter a supernatural rest as we believe the truth of who we are in Christ and who He is in us. Jesus is coming back for a pure and spotless bride. Because of Jesus and the finished work on the cross, we already are pure and spotless, not based on our works, but based on the completed work of Christ on the cross!

Meditate on this: *"For it is God who is at work in you, both to will and to work for His good pleasure." Philippians 2:13 NASV*

"What actually took place is this: I tried keeping rules and working my head off to please God, and it didn't work. So I quit being a "law man" so I could be God's man. Christ's life in me showed me how, and enabled me to do it. I identified myself completely with Him. Indeed, I have been crucified with Christ. My ego is no longer central. It is no

8

longer important that I appear righteous before you or have your good opinion, and I am no longer driven to impress God. Christ lives in me. The life you see me living is not 'mine', but it is lived by faith in the Son of God, who loved me and gave Himself for me. I am not going back on that."
Galatians 2:19-21 MSG

Prayer: Father, please, open the eyes of my heart. Give me a greater revelation of who You are in me. Heal my heart. Set me free. Give me joy based in Your love for me. I turn to You, Father. I'm asking You to help me trust You to filter things away from my life and heart that doesn't align with Your Words and how You already see me righteous in You, because of Jesus.

In Jesus Name I pray, Amen.

Angela Steele

DAY 4

Significant in Jesus

(Part Four in the *Identifying with Jesus' Love Series*)

Who Christ is in me is the most significant thing about me. Jesus has already made me significant, based on what He has already finished on the Cross. As a Christian, *who* do I identify with on a daily basis? Do I identify with people's words or do I identify with my Savior's words? If I weigh people's opinions, more than God's opinion, then I have chosen to place people above God, which is idolatry. Worshipping people rather than Jesus leads to a wasteland. With Jesus as my core and center of my life, my significance comes from Him, not a fickle friend. With Jesus as my core, my significance comes from Him, not how my children respond to me. With Jesus as my core, my significance comes from Him, not my title, ranking, or status.

Once I started awakening to the truth that I am significant in Jesus, I not only began to see myself differently, but I began to see other people differently as well. My mind still needs renewing, but because I know God loves me all the time, I find my identity in Him, and my need to have people validate me has lessened. If people aren't viewing me the way I know God views me, then their opinion doesn't matter. Jesus validates me, not people.

As I began understanding my significance in Jesus, the amount of disagreements and arguments in my life has lessened. Why? Not because circumstances or people have changed, but because I'm not looking to them for validation. Their thoughts and actions do not define who I am. Jesus defines who I am. I follow my Creator's voice.

I am significant and qualified in Him because of my right standing with Him, because of Him. It's all Him! Jesus trumpets us as significant! Let's identify with God's Word! We are valued, accepted, respected, and a loved daughters of the King!

Meditate on this: *"How precious also are Thy thoughts to me, O God! How vast is the sum of them! If I should count them, they would outnumber the sand. When I awake, I am still with Thee." Psalm 139:17, 18 NASV*

Summing it all up, friends, I'd say you'll do best by filling your minds and meditating on things true, noble, reputable, authentic, compelling, gracious—the best, not the worst; the beautiful, not the ugly; things to praise, not to curse. Put into practice what you learned from me, what you heard and saw and realized. Do that, and God, who makes everything work together, will work you into his most excellent harmonies." Philippians 4:8,9 MSG

Prayer: Jesus, renew our minds to our significance in You. You paid a great price for us, and we rest in the truth that Your loving eye is ever upon us, and Your hand guides us into each hour of our day. Affirm in our hearts that You love us simply because we are Yours, covered and wrapped in Your Love. In Jesus' Name we pray, Amen

Angela Steele

DAY 5

"God is Not a Man"

While listening to a sermon on YouTube by Bill Winston, my spirit was ignited and joy flooded my soul. I erupted in praise as I fellowshipped with God. I found myself repeating and emphasizing a particular verse Mr. Winston had passionately quoted, "God is not a man that he should lie…" when suddenly, my spirit caught the revelation of the verse; it had a profound effect on me. God illuminated His light where darkness lurked, and gave me a new perspective.

Logically, I knew that God was not a man, He is a Spirit, but spiritually I wasn't connecting to it. The disconnection impaired my relationship with God and it was evident in my life. The disconnection was brought about by lack of trust; unbelief resided in my heart. As a result, my life was stagnant for years, it seemed that I had taken up residency in the valley of doom and I could not get out, tried as hard as I did. During these times I felt rejected and abandoned, I felt God was partial and I was the least of His children, because others were receiving their blessings and I was not. What I failed to realize is that the problem was I all along.

Let me try and explain.

For many years the spirit of unbelief-a lack of trust in God plagued me. Anger and resentment had significantly dominated my heart and it made me cold hearted; immune to vulnerability.

My biological father and several key male figures emotionally wounded me throughout my life. These painful memories and wounds were embedded deep within me and they crippled me emotionally and hampered my ability to form emotional, intimate and lasting relationships.

My history with men tainted my opinion of them. They were liars and users, who were not to be trusted: they represented disappointments, rejections, broken promises, abandonment, and sorrow. My relationship with God was directly impacted by my relationship with men.

Through the years these unresolved issues were a thorn between God and I. Every time I would believe God for something I had asked Him for, there was a constant annoying little voice off to the left side of my brain reminding me of all the disappointments I had endured from broken promises. I was unable to move beyond a superficial relationship with God because I didn't trust Him to keep His promises. Lack of trust put distance between God and me and it prevented me from developing an intimate relationship with Him. Communication with Him was difficult, it was a struggle to find the right words when I prayed, I had a hard time vocalizing my thoughts and desires, and it impeded my ability to hear from Him.

The revelation of God, not being a man, gave me clarity and put everything into perspective as to why I was not seeing the manifestation of His blessings in my life. Along with the spirit of unbelief, my faith level was at an all-time low, this counteracted my confessions and held up God's promises; I could not receive what I was not expecting.

Throughout life turbulences I remained steadfast, I had an insatiable appetite for an intimate relationship with God and I perused Him. Every time I turned around, it seemed like I was bombarded by other people's testimonies proclaiming God's goodness and faithfulness. They told stories of how God answered their prayers in miraculous, timely and generous ways. Their manner of communication with God seemed to flow effortlessly and that would trigger a painful response from me. I was overcome by grief as my heart ached with pain and I would burst out crying; I felt abandoned.

I would often cry out, "God what's wrong with me? Why don't I know you like that?" I longed to know Him like they did, to have that connection and intimacy they had with Him.

I thank God for His faithful love. He heard and responded to my cry. I came to understand that my inability to connect with Him was predicated on my lack of trust. God helped me to face my issues and as I did, it made room for Him to come closer. His words began to come alive in me and I learned to trust Him. I began to consciously implement his words in my life regardless of my circumstances, senses, and experience. During the process my faith was restored, Praise God! As I continued seeking Him, I saw my relationship with Him changed radically and intimacy between us increased.

One night while I was reading **11 Chronicles 1:7 (NKJV)** "...**Ask what I shall give thee.**"

It struck me, if He told Solomon that, He is also telling me the same. I challenged God, saying, "I didn't hear you ask me this question audibly, but it's in your word, so I am applying it to me. In a roundabout way I think I was saying, "If you are not a respecter of person, then you will answer me too." It was a test; unbelief was trying to creep back in my mind.

What I was unaware of, is that He had answered me, I didn't make the connection until a couple of days later. God blessed me by fulfilling a desire that was buried within me after many disappointments of trying to achieve it. God was faster than the enemy. He showed me by renouncing unbelief I could receive from Him. Trusting God enabled me to give and receive freely, "Who God set free, is free indeed." I experienced God's generosity on a level that I had never before; He came through for me in a great way and made good on His promises.

The revelation that "He was not a man" totally terminated the disconnection and put unbelief to rest. In that moment, as the revelation was unfolding I felt a shift took place; the connection was severed, and separation took place. In the spirit I saw God separate from man. He stood above to my right and man was below on my left. His hands were outstretched towards me and He had a smile on His face.

I finally saw God for who He really is; He who stands apart from man in all his Glory. "He is not a man" is forever solidified in my mind-soul and spirit. God is God all by Himself.

Meditate on this: *"God is not a man, that he should lie; neither the son of man, that he should repent: hath he said, and shall he not do it? Or hath he spoken, and shall he not make it good?"* Numbers 23:19 (KJV)

Prayer: Lord, I know you are not a man, and I thank you that you are no respecter of person. It's your will for your children to know you as the generous father that you are. Your words are always true. You will not withhold any good things from us if we walk uprightly before you, put you first, and seek your face. I pray that your children will not rely on their senses, intellect, emotions, circumstances or experiences, for you do not operate as men do. I pray that they will submit their will to you and if there is any blockage in their lives, please show them as you did me and remove it in Jesus name, Amen.

Annmarie Givans

DAY 6

Answered Prayer

My dad was dying. Day after day I sat beside his hospital bed and watched as he struggled to breathe. I was heartbroken, but it was the fear that consumed my thoughts and at times rendered me helpless. Fear that I had inherited the blood disease that had developed into leukemia and was killing my dad at an alarming rate? No. Fear that I wouldn't be able to handle his death? No, although, both of these were concerns, the fear that rendered me helpless was that my dad would spend eternity in Hell.

My dad was a kind, honest, hard-working, all- around good guy. Unfortunately, being good does not keep one from Hell. So for years I prayed for his salvation. In addition, I purchased him a Bible and invited him to church. I knew that my paternal grandparents were strong Christians and had raised my father in church, but again, that does not give one a pass into heaven. All I knew for certain was that for as long as I could remember, my mother got up on Sunday morning, dressed my sister and me and we headed to church; Dad headed to work. I don't think I ever saw him read a

Bible nor do I remember hearing him pray. Not that church attendance, reading the Bible or praying aloud gains one entrance into heaven either but they are outward appearances of a Christian; and absent in my dad's life.

Months before Dad was diagnosed with leukemia, he mentioned that he and my step-mother had begun attending church. I was so excited but continued to pray. Then he became sick and was hospitalized. During the hospital stay a friend of his visited and asked Dad if all was settled between him and the Lord. Dad replied that he had taken care of all that years ago when he was a child. I should have been shouting for joy but I still was not at peace so I continued to pray.

The disease continued rendering this once energetic, hard-working individual helpless. One day as he lay sleeping, I picked up a Christian publication and a story caught my interest. The author of the story described how her grandmother believed that when a family member was taken to heaven God sent a butterfly as a message to the family. I remember bowing my head and pouring out my concern to the Lord. I even told Him that I could use a butterfly message letting me know that when Dad left me, he would be in Heaven. Suddenly, I began to feel a peace and with each prayer over the next few days the peace grew stronger. In fact, I told the Lord that I probably didn't need a butterfly after all.

And then it happened, Dad breathed his last breath on earth. The next day as we were traveling to make funeral arrangements I thought I saw a butterfly. Then later that night, I opened a magazine and there were three pages of butterflies. That was just the beginning. Everywhere I went the next few days there was a butterfly. With each sighting I would be filled with peace and thanksgiving. It was almost as if the Lord was saying, "See I heard your prayer and answered. And your Dad is right here with Me and we both love you!"

I realize that no one can be absolutely certain about another's salvation. But I truly believe that the Lord answered my prayers for Dad and that when I take my last breath on earth, both my heavenly and earthly fathers will welcome me into Heaven.

Dad has been gone for sixteen years now and as my thoughts travel back to that time I realize that the Lord used that situation to teach me a few valuable lessons: He is always available to listen to our concerns, His peace surpasses all understanding, we need to live our lives in such a way that our loved ones never have to worry about our eternal destination, life here on earth is short, and He does answer our prayers!

Meditate on this: *"Come to me, all you who are weary and burdened, and I will give you rest."* Matthew 11:29

"Peace I leave with you; my peace I give you. I do not give to you as the world gives. Do not let your hearts be troubled and do not be afraid." John 14:27

"For God so loved the world that he gave his one and only Son, that whoever believes in him shall not perish but have eternal life." John 3:16

"Ask, and it shall be given you; seek, and ye shall find; knock, and it shall be opened unto you: For every one that asketh receiveth; and he that seeketh findeth; and to him that knocketh it shall be opened." Matthew 7:7-8

Prayer: Dear Father, thank You for loving me so much that You sent Your son to die in my place. Thank You for always listening to my fears and granting me peace. Thank You for teaching me Your ways and answering my prayers. And Father thank You for the butterflies, I didn't need them but with each sighting I felt Your love and still do.

Karen White

DAY 7

Empty Arms

My husband and I produced three children in less than four years. In fact, within a fifteen-year span there were eleven children born amongst our siblings; not including those born to cousins and friends. No one ever discussed timing of pregnancies, ovulation, or fertility; for the obvious reason, there was no need. I guess we took Genesis 9:7 (NIV) literally. "As for you, be fruitful and increase in number; multiply on the earth and increase upon it."

In the year 1999, while others feared the loss of life as we know it, worrying about computer crashes and all that the new century would bring, our family was busy planning a wedding. Our oldest daughter married and not only did we gain a son-in-law but we became grandparents to a precious four-year-old boy. Little did we know that a year later we would embark on a journey, one that spanned eight years and brought many trials and heartbreaks.

We were so excited the day our daughter announced they had decided to have a baby. I immediately began shopping for baby items. After all we were going to have a grandbaby in nine months, right? Only nine months later not only did we not have a baby, there wasn't even one in "the oven" as my grandparents would say.

By this time most of their friends and family knew they were trying to conceive so they were given lots of advice that ranged from her gaining weight to standing on her head after they made love. The advice wasn't limited to our daughter, our son-in-law was told to change his underwear style and use ice to name a few words of wisdom. In addition, to the "friendly advice" our daughter had researched and discovered a few more techniques. However, none of the techniques worked, so she consulted her gynecologist.

The gynecologist advised them to take a break and after a period of time if she still was not pregnant he would begin running test. The test revealed that she had endometriosis. Her gynecologist performed surgery to rid her body of the disease and informed her that she would conceive within six months. The next six months passed in two week intervals; ovulation test then pregnancy test. Six months became a year and a year became three.

In January of 2005, our son-in-law was deployed to Afghanistan. Although the separation was hard for them, it did relieve the pressure of trying to conceive. It was during this time that the gynecologist suggested that our daughter begin taking birth control pills to assist with the endometriosis that had returned. Later, a second surgery would be performed to again remove the damage caused by endometriosis.

In the spring of 2007, her gynecologist referred her to a fertility specialist. Thus, another type of struggle began within our daughter's heart. She felt God had told her she would have a baby but was she taking the matter out of His hands by proceeding? Should she just be patient and wait on Him? After much prayer and many discussions, she decided to consult the fertility specialist. The specialist prescribed a fertility drug and ran additional test. The next few months revolved around side effects of the fertility drug, ovulation and pregnancy test. At the end of the year, the fertility specialist referred them to his partner, who had more experience.

Our family began the New Year filled with hope. However, it soon became an emotional roller coaster. The fertility specialist recommended In Vitro Fertilization (IVF) and "Liquid Gold", as the medication is called due to its cost. I would like to point out that not only are these medications expense and not covered by most insurance, they also have severe side effects. After a month of hormones gone wild while taking the medication, my daughter had a sonogram which revealed that her left ovary was enlarged; possible due to a cyst or endometriosis. The real problem however, was that there were only 3 or 4 follicles present. The specialist recommended that she continue taking the medication until the end of the month when another sonogram would be administered.

At the end of the month and additional medication she should have had lots of follicles. Unfortunately, there was only one present. The concerned look on the specialist face spoke volumes. He informed us that he wanted to check her estrogen level and would call with the results in a few days. He explained that unless the estrogen level was sufficient, a choice would have to be made. After outlining their choices, he recommended that considering her age (she was now 35) and her history she should consider adoption.

As we walked to the parking lot our hearts were heavy. But it only took one follicle, right? There was still hope, slight but it was there. We said goodbye and headed in opposite directions and then within a few hours I received the call. The test results were back. My daughter's estrogen level, that should be close to two hundred, was at twenty.

While still reeling from this latest blow, my daughter received a phone call a few weeks later. A friend of a relative was asked to adopt a baby. However, since she had recently adopted two children she was unable to take on another child. She had called my son-in-law's cousin in hopes of her adopting the baby. Unfortunately, due to a family situation, she too was unable to take on the child but instantly thought of my daughter. Thus, with one phone call, hope sprang in our hearts. I can't go into all the details but after weeks of trying to get all the paperwork in order, the mother decided to keep the baby girl.

My daughter and son-in-law were heart broken. They had been allowed to visit, hold the baby and had taken pictures with her. They had a name chosen, a nursery set up and a car seat mounted in the back seat. But it wasn't to be, it would have been very easy after eight years of physical, emotional, and financial trials during this journey for them to become bitter. And I will admit the question "why" came up more than a few times. Why were so many others; some of whom were young, unmarried, and totally unprepared to be parents been blessed with children and my daughter was not.

It is not our place however, to question and only God knows the reason why. I am proud to say that although my daughter's arms are empty her heart is full. With many prayers and turning it over to God (more than once), she is the favorite aunt to her nieces and nephews, the "other mother" to many of her stepson's friends, and the mentor to the church's youth. Her life is full and productive and God has blessed her in many ways.

Meditate on this: *"For I know the plans I have for you," declares the Lord, "plans to prosper you and not to harm you, plans to give you hope and a future."* Jeremiah 29:11 NIV

Prayer: Dear Father, I thank you for our family. I ask that we always remember Your plan is best. Father, there are other young women who desire to hold a child in their arms but for some reason their arms remain empty. I ask that You surround them with love, provide them with strength, and comfort them during the struggle. It is in Your name I ask, Amen.

Karen White

DAY 8

Test of Faith

This all started in 2012; it seemed like everyone was saying they had been diagnosed with cancer. Just hearing the word, cancer, made me uneasy. In September of 2012, my life was shaken up a little. I started to smell a foul odor, and I did not know why I had this odor. The odor was getting stronger by the day, and so one day after work, I decided to examine my breasts. Underneath my right breast, I had a small mole that had been there for years. I noticed that the mole was gone. It had been replaced by a soft, grey looking bump that had pus oozing out of it. Now my mind is running a thousand miles not knowing what's going on. I continued examining my breast but did not feel a lump. I grabbed my computer looking for answers, but that wasn't helping.

The following day at work, I told my coworkers what was going. I was scared (usually, I'm the one that encourages everyone and talks about faith, but not this time). Then my coworker that was a breast cancer survivor spoke up. She said, "Kim you don't have cancer but make your appointment now and when you finish think about what you often tell us." I made my appointment but still had little faith. I didn't tell my family what was going on at this time, instead I called a church member and my prayer warriors because my brain was numb to anything. They prayed and gave me scriptures to read and meditate on because my appointment was in two days. Finally, the appointment day arrived, and as the nurse got ready to examine me, I told her that I had a terrible odor (this odor was so strong it made me sick in the stomach). She said the results would take five days, but then I got a call telling me to call the office (it was not what I wanted to hear). She told me a spot was found on the right side and I needed to come back in two weeks, now two weeks was a long time to worry. At that time my life seemed dark. The tears were flowing nonstop, my brain racing; how do I tell my sons, my family? When I got home, the Bible was on the bed and I started reading. My friend called, she is a preaching Evangelist, and she laughed when I told her the news. This is what she said, "You do not have cancer, get your faith back. At this time, I had to decide. My boys were finally home and I told them the news, which they took well. Next, I contacted my mom and my five siblings. While waiting in my storm I started meditating on God's word, my faith kicked in. I walked down the hall declaring these words, "If I have cancer I will beat it, it will not beat me. God you have shown me my Vision, I will stand before many speaking, so this is not happening, I will see my youngest graduate from high school!" When I say my faith kicked in, my Lord my Lord is all I can say. My second appointment was going to be in one day, my oldest son said, "Momma I will go with you," but I said, "no son I have this". The next day I was examined and afterwards as I got dressed, the nurse came back and said, "Ma'am you need to get undressed again. The doctor needs to do another examination". So I went in for another examination with the doctor eventually said, "NO CANCER!" Apparently, the spot with the foul smell was a highly infected hair cyst, and he advised that I could let the remaining infection drain or have it removed. I opted to have it removed, called my doctor and it was removed the same day. In hindsight, I realize it was a test of my Faith.

No matter what you are going through never let your faith waver. *"Truly I tell you, if you have faith as small as a mustard seed, you can say to this mountain, 'Move from here to there; and it will move. Nothing will be impossible for you."* Matthew 17:20

Meditate on this: *"Trust in the Lord with all your heart and lean not on your own understanding, in all your ways submit to him, and he will make your paths straight.* Proverbs 3:5

Prayer: Father in Heaven, today and every day I choose to believe that you are working behind the scene on my behalf. I trust that you have a good plan for me and that You are leading and guiding my every step. Help me to stand strong in any situation I may encounter while holding on to Faith. In Jesus name Amen.

Kim White- Donaby

DAY 9

Learning to be Still

Around 2010, I was invited to attend an event called, 100 Ladies to Christ. This was something I was looking forward to doing. Well that Friday night I decided to get my hair done because the drive was only 4 hours away. Now all this time I was feeling great. When I got home everything was still good until I started walking up my stairs. Suddenly, I broke out in a sweat, I wasn't able to get my words out and I had some pain in abdomen, so I decided if I laid down it would help. As I got to my bedroom, I decided to change into something more comfortable, but it never happened. Clear fluids started gushing out of me down my legs, my eyes were getting bigger and the pain was unbearable. The pain was so unbearable I was only able to take a few steps before I fell across the bed shaking my head from left to right. Still I wasn't calling for help until I heard a voice out of nowhere say, "You will die if you don't get help. My cell phone was near so I called my sister who is a registered nurse, but I was barely able to speak. She called the ambulance and said she would meet me at the hospital. While going to the hospital, I started praying that the pain would leave, I was barely able to walk. My body was so weak they started checking my vital signs right away. Now I don't have a blood pressure issues, but my blood pressure that night was 190/100 because of all the pain. They put me in a room trying to figure out what was wrong, they took my blood (scared of needles) but stuck me wrong so my arm started swelling up with air bubble. I was really praying now. They wanted to give me morphine for pain but I'm allergic to pain medication so I declined. The results came back; I had a ruptured cyst and the good news was it wasn't blood and they did not have to do surgery. The doctor said it never happens like that, and I said, "Prayer changes things. Now can I leave?" He said, "Leave?" I said, "Yes, because some people are expecting me to speak at an event around noon on Saturday. He said, "You can't go out of town, you need to rest." The pain was still bad but I needed to go and speak at the event. Finally, they sent me home with some Tylenol and a bedrest prescription.

While resting in bed and watching the news, I saw a horrible accident. Several cars were in the accident along with an 18 wheeler that was carrying flammable liquids. The interstate was being shut down going the exact way I would have been going. As I watched, the tears started coming. God was trying to get me to be still because I was going that way. All I could think about was what some people always tell me, they often say I do too much, and never rest. That could have been me in that terrible accident. God used the illness to get my attention and cause me to be still. When I wasn't able to attend the event, I was hurt but I later realized the reason. I realized that it happened for several reasons; I needed to take care of my health better and learn to be still at times. So if it hadn't been for the pain I might not be here today. I often look back on that situation because I never had any pain until that day. I do know a few days before I was due to set out, I had an uneasy feeling about the trip, something was telling me not to go but the stubborn person I am refused to listen or be still. When God says, "Be still," be still and listen.

Meditate on this: *"Be still, and know that I am God. I will be exalted among the nations. I will be exalted in the earth."* Psalm 46:10

Prayer: Father in Heaven, today and every day I ask that You give me patience to be still and remember, in everything I do, that You are God. In Jesus name Amen.

Kim White-Donaby

Day 10

Testimony of Love for God's People

Sometimes in our Christian walk, God will bring a very special someone into your life who will encourage and bless you. Well I have been very blessed by one such person, her name is Trisha. God also gives us children who are very precious, well me and my husband have two grown up boys Andrew and Matthew. Andrew the eldest is special needs and has high functioning autism. This has meant lots of hospital and doctors' appointments; these were mainly easy to do but there was one such appointment that presented a real challenge. It was a 2-hour train journey to a London hospital which would have been fine but at the time I was occasionally getting panic attacks, so being stuck on a crowded train for two hours was not going to be easy. I prayed hard that God would keep me calm and give me the strength and courage I needed to get through the day. It started well but then the train began to fill up with people and my anxiety rose but just as I continued to pray we pulled into the next station and more people got on. Suddenly this tall slim lady sat down beside me and the first thing she did was get out her Bible and wow, did that put me at peace. We had a wonderful chat and she really encouraged me. Four stops later, she got off. It was only two stops before ours and she gave me her number so we could stay in touch and we did.

A couple of years later, Andrew went in for quite a big operation on his throat and he text Trisha and asked her to pray for him and she did. She also gave Andrew Psalm 91 which gave him such peace and it's been our favourite Bible verse since.

"He who dwells in the secret place of the Most High Shall abide under the shadow of the Almighty. I will say of the LORD, "He is my refuge and my fortress; My God, in Him I will trust." **Psalm 91:1-2 (NKJV)**

The operation went really well and the nursing staff were surprised how good Andrew came out of the Anaesthetic.

We continued to stay in touch and some years later at the age of ten Andrew gave His life to the Lord and was baptized. Trish of course came down to see him and in an open prayer time for him she brought a prophecy out. Andrew has always had a talent and love for music and even played a song at his baptism. She said "Andrew's music would go throughout all the world bringing healing and deliverance." That prophecy has now come true but what is so absolutely amazing is, at the time of his baptism there was no internet for common use and I struggled to see how it would go so far. I thought he would be doing a lot of travelling, but now he has his own website and YouTube channel and is creating and singing some powerful songs.

Prayer: I give Praise and glory to the wonders of God and thank him for sending such wonderful people into my life. I pray that this testimony will touch someone's heart and encourage them to trust Him in every situation of their lives and that they may fill their lives with love and peace and that God send them that special person into their lives Amen and God bless you all

Julie Clark

DAY 11

Look Up!

In the summer of 1987, I was enjoying a summer's day at the beach with a few of my co-workers and their small children and my boss at his beach house in beautiful Edisto Beach, South Carolina. The day was gorgeous, warm and sunny but not too hot. The sky was a bright blue and it was windy. My son and I were walking near the pier and Jacob asked me, "Mama, can I go play over there with the others?" A few of the children were splashing in the ankle-deep water. "Ok, Jacob, but don't go close to the pier." The reason for my warning was because my son wore glasses and could not see anything without them. He, of course, had them on at the time and did not want to take them off. I knew the water might splash up on his face as it crashed against the pier and the glasses might be knocked off his face. Jacob, delighted at my answer, nodded and ran over to where the other children were playing. I walked on for a few yards, looking out over the water.

My husband and I had been concerned about our finances, as my job did not pay a lot. We did have good medical benefits…just not vision insurance. In a few moments I heard my son cry out, "Mama!" I looked around and he was running toward me, saying, "Mama, I lost my glasses." "The water knocked them off my face and they fell in the water." He was looking up at me with sad, anxious eyes.

"Ok, well, take me to where you were standing," I was hoping desperately that he had not been too far into the water and that maybe…just maybe…they would have just been covered by the wet sand. However, when he pointed to the area where he had been standing, I saw that, sure enough, he had been right by the pier where the water was churning and the waves were pounding the boards. I felt so dejected and frustrated. My heart sank. Jacob's glasses were practically new and we did not have any money to replace them right now. He could not go without them. What would I do? I looked everywhere in the area, wading out into the water, and even up very close to the pier where the water was splashing up onto my clothes. I didn't see any glasses. In fact, I really couldn't see anything because the water was so turbulent. Then I thought to myself, *I will pray*.

I looked up into that bright blue sky, stood perfectly still, and closed my eyes, "God," I said aloud, "You know that we do not have the money to replace my son's glasses…please help me."

I looked down to see the water receding and there, on the top of my feet, neatly folded, were my son's glasses—not even scratched. I smiled, "Thank you, Lord!" I reached down and grabbed them quickly before another wave came crashing over my feet.

In this life, we will face many trials—some small, some huge. Our day may start off wonderful and pleasant with blue skies and no problems in sight. We may be enjoying ourselves and the world around us but just as quickly, our day can go dark and problems can cause us to lose our focus. We may feel helpless in our situation, unable and afraid to make even a simple decision. There is someone we can always turn to. Just like my son came crying to me to help him when he lost his glasses—and knew he could not find them on his own--I remembered to ask the Lord for help. I had gone with my son back to the pier to see if I could find the glasses and with God's help, as I cried out to Him, I was helped.

Meditate on this: *"Let us therefore come boldly to the throne of grace, that we may obtain mercy, and find grace to help in time of need."* Hebrews 4:16

Prayer: Dear Lord, You can hear our heart's cry when we call on You in our desperation. When we have the courage and faith to pray to You and tell you exactly how much we need You, You always hear your children and answer us. May we remember to cry out, knowing that You are listening for our voice!

Marilyn Smith

DAY 12

Nothing Missing Nothing Stolen

My uncle was returning to the UK after a three week visit to Nigeria. That morning, as he prepared to leave for the airport, he remembered he was yet to deliver a parcel for a friend in the UK who had sent him to her brother and his wife. Before we got into the car he handed me the parcel and asked me to deliver it for him. The parcel was for Yinka and Nkechi and their address was somewhere on Allen Avenue, Ikeja. As it wasn't far from the airport, I decided that once we dropped him off, my cousins and I (the escort party) would go and deliver the package and that was exactly what we did.

When we arrived at that part of Allen Avenue though, we noticed the building numbers were a little mixed up so we began to make enquiries and were directed to an office where a lady named Nkechi worked. This Nkechi had a fiancé named Yinka. Now because the parcel was addressed to Yinka and Nkechi and the number of this office was the same as the one written on the parcel, we handed it over and left. Now you can imagine my shock when three months later I met the real Yinka. My uncle had sent him to me with a parcel and I mentioned giving a parcel to his fiancée, Nkechi, three months earlier. Well, he gave me a blank stare. He had no clue what I was on about. He was not engaged to Nkechi, Nkechi was his wife and they had been married for a few years. He also said that his office was directly opposite the office where we had taken the parcel. Oh my goodness! I knew I had really blown it. Wasn't there an uneasy feeling that suddenly came over me just before I handed the parcel to that woman? What was I to do now? Immediately, the Holy Spirit instructed me to go back to her and ask her to return the parcel. Go back and ask for the parcel, after three months? A parcel I so generously handed to her, not like I was coerced or anything like that? I would not have obeyed except that I was certain God was behind the voice. Well, when I got to the office, surprise, surprise, another company was occupying the building! Now, I almost passed out. Thankfully, one of the staff knew where the other company had moved and I was given the address. When I arrived, Nkechi was out on official duty so I waited. After about an hour she returned and I introduced myself and wasted no time letting her know the reason for my visit. I did not know what to expect really. When I was done talking, she smiled, walked over to her desk and pulled out the parcel, intact. According to her she had no idea who sent the parcel and when she asked her fiancé, Yinka, he didn't know either and so they decided that she leave the parcel in her office in case we came back for it. She added however, that having waited all these months she had decided only that morning to take the parcel home with her and keep the items or give them out. I heaved a sigh of relief. "Thank you Jesus" I muttered under my breath as I rushed out of her office with the parcel clutched to my chest.

I am grateful to God that I was finally able to deliver the parcel to the right Yinka and Nkechi. God kept that package intact and protected my integrity. He alone is worthy to be praised.

Meditate on this: *"And now I exhort you to be of good cheer: for there shall be no loss..."* Acts 27:22

Prayer: Father I thank you because you are mindful of me and as such I suffer no loss.

Eturuvie Erebor

DAY 13

His Blood Runs in My Veins

A few years ago, I was travelling to the UK from Nigeria and this was in the very early stage of my pregnancy. When I arrived I was in pains and I assumed it was caused by the stress of the journey and the fact that I lifted my very heavy suitcases all by myself. I was in pains for the next two days following my arrival. Finally, on the third day I decided to go in to the Accident & Emergency unit to be seen by a doctor. While I talked to the doctor I felt the need to explain that the journey from Nigeria plus the lifting of my heavy suitcases may have hurt me in some way hence the pains in my lower abdomen but for some bizarre reason he thought I must be manifesting malaria symptoms and decided to run some tests. I was informed that if the test results revealed a trace of malaria parasite in my blood I would not be allowed to leave the hospital. I thought he was a quack who was leaving the real issues and chasing a shadow but I consented to my blood being taken and tested.

As I waited for the results I kept thinking of the vigil service in church that night and how much I wanted to be in attendance. I certainly did not want to be quarantined and miss the service. At this point the Lord reminded me of a testimony. A brother in my church had attended a job interview and was certain he had pleased the panel and so was completely blown away when he was told that even though he had performed well, he was not the one they had chosen for the job. Then he remembered the Scripture that says that wherever the sole of our feet shall tread has been given to us for a possession. He asked to use their restroom and once inside, he took of his shoes, placed his bare feet on the ground and claimed that place as his. On his way out of the building, he was stopped at reception and advised that the information given to him earlier should be disregarded as it was an error and he was actually the one they had chosen. As soon as I was reminded of the testimony, I rose to my feet and asked to use the hospital's restroom. Once I was inside, I took off my shoes and placed my bare feet on the ground and took possession of the place. I commanded everything and everyone there to work in my favour. I remembered also that Jesus is the vine and we are the branches and in the natural, no branch has life of itself but what it receives from the vine and for that reason when a branch is broken off, it withers and dies. I decreed that because I was the branch, I had no life of my own, no blood of my own, but the blood of the vine (Jesus) and so if there was no malaria parasite in His blood they would find no malaria parasite in my blood which was in reality, His blood. As I stepped out of the rest room, the doctor approached me. He had the test results with him. There was no trace of malaria parasite in my blood.

Meditate on this: *"I am the vine, ye are the branches: He that abideth in me, and I in him, the same bringeth forth much fruit: for without me ye can do nothing."* John 15:5

"Every place that the sole of your foot shall tread upon, that have I given unto you, as I said unto Moses." Joshua 1:3

"Every place whereon the soles of your feet shall tread shall be yours: from the wilderness and Lebanon, from the river, the river Euphrates, even unto the uttermost sea shall your coast be." Deuteronomy 11:24

Prayer: Father give to me every place where the sole of my feet shall tread. And help me to live and walk in the reality that the blood of Jesus flows in my veins.

Eturuvie Erebor

DAY 14

His Blood Runs in My Veins (Part Two)

When I began my antenatal classes with my midwife, she immediately wanted to know everything about me including health challenges in my maternal and paternal families. I informed her that my mother's family suffered from diabetes and so she made an appointment for me to go in to the hospital to have a test. Immediately the devil paid me a little visit to remind me that my mother had been pregnant with me, her first child, when she was discovered to have diabetes. And here I was, pregnant with my first child, I could expect the test result to reveal that I had diabetes. He also proceeded to remind me that diabetes had led to the untimely deaths of my mother's parents, my mother and her siblings. But as he spoke, the Scripture came alive in my heart. And I remembered that Jesus said, *"I am the vine and ye are the branches"*.

Then a day or two before I went for the tests, some 'well-meaning friends' tried to 'assure me'. According to them, many women without a history of diabetes in their families suffer from pregnancy induced diabetes which usually terminates at the birth of their babies. I knew it was the devil speaking through them so I rejected every word they spoke and held on to God's word. As far as I was concerned I had changed families when I became born again so the negative patterns in my maternal family had no power over me.

I went for the test and to God be the glory, three days later, I got a letter in the post that said they were pleased to inform me that I had no trace of diabetes and my body was breaking down sugar well.

Meditate on this: "*I am the vine, ye are the branches: He that abideth in me, and I in him, the same bringeth forth much fruit: for without me ye can do nothing.*" John 15:5

Prayer: Father, I believe that Jesus is the vine and that I am the branch. I believe that just as the vine gives its life to the branch, Jesus gives His life to me. I receive that life, the life that is free of sickness and disease. In Jesus' name. Amen.

Eturuvie Erebor

Day 15

His Blessing Abides

During my service year I had a huge accommodation challenge that went on for about two months and it was during this period that I came in contact with my present place of worship. I still remember the first vigil I attended, it was tagged, Hosanna Night which could also mean a night of praise and we were asked to praise God for our needs. I thought that was weird, I was used to asking God for my needs but I'd never heard of praising Him for my needs. I thought it was a bit awkward to be praising for something He had not given me. Anyway I obeyed the pastor's instructions, I wrote out what I wanted on a piece of paper, a decent accommodation being top on the list, and I put the paper on the ground (still following the pastor's instructions) and danced on that list all night.

On Saturday evening, I went out to visit a family friend who I had lost contact with for my years and then suddenly run into again in Abuja. They had known of my struggle to get a place and during this visit she informed me that her husband had secured a BQ room for me in Fort IBB, Asokoro. Now, I had no idea they were even looking for a place for me. She said her husband was unhappy because they were unable to accommodate me at their home and so he had requested Army Headquarters (he was an officer with the Nigerian Army) to provide him a place for a family friend who was in Abuja for her service year and had no place to stay. Well, Army Headquarters had a lot of unoccupied rooms in the barracks and they gave him the keys to one of the rooms. It was indeed an answer to my praise.

On Monday evening I moved into my new place. Less than a month later my family friend was sent out of Nigeria on peace keeping mission and one night I received a letter from Army Headquarters asking me to vacate the room within 48 hours or be thrown out. I panicked my family friend who got me the place was away in Liberia who would bail me out? Then the Lord answered my question with one of His? Was it Colonel Brume (not real name) who got this place for you? Immediately I said, "No". Then the Lord asked, "How did you get this place? I replied that I had praised Him for it and He used my family friend to provide it for me. So the Lord instructed me to put the letter from Army Headquarters on the ground and dance over it as I had done in church during the Hosanna Night service. I obeyed and went to bed.

Two days later, very early in the morning, I was woken by a bang on my door. I jumped out of bed and opened the door to face three fierce looking soldiers who wanted to know why I had failed to move. I told them I didn't have a place to move to and they assured me that once they threw my things out I would have a place to go. Without another word to me, they turned and began to bang on my neighbour's door. I explained to them that he had left for work as he usually leaves early. Before I was done with an explanation of my neighbour's whereabouts, they had broken the door and began to move his things out. I stood watching in horror because I knew I was next in line for the unpleasant experience. In less than ten minutes they'd cleared the room and turned in my direction and I half expected one of them to grab me by the arm and shove me aside but to my surprise they marched off and until I finished my youth service and moved out about ten months later nobody from Army Headquarters came there again to bother me. This God is awesome.

Meditate on this: *"I know that, whatsoever God doeth, it shall be for ever: nothing can be put to it, nor any thing taken from it: and God doeth it, that men should fear before him."* Ecclesiastes 3:14

Prayer: Father I thank you because your blessings in my life shall abide. No one can add to or take away from that which you have done.

Eturuvie Erebor

Day 16

A Badly Written CV

A few years ago I returned to live in the UK in obedience to God's instructions. I was not off the plane before I began to send out my CV in search of a job. I was constantly told me that I would have difficulties getting a job. I was reminded me that the last five years I had lived and worked in Nigeria and had no recent UK work experience and as such would not be able to get a job. Some suggested that I re-write my CV and exclude my experience outside the UK and then others, who claimed to know about professional CV writing, said my CV was badly written and gave me tips on how to re-write my CV. But God was not going to share His glory with anyone so all I got from the new CV was a cleaning job in some very high profile, members only, restaurant. I was very broke at this point and really desperate and the yearly pay was quite impressive for a cleaning job so I took it grudgingly.

I spent all of the hours of my first shift complaining to God. He could hear me so I murmured endlessly. "Why did you bring me to London? Why didn't you just leave me in

Nigeria? I had a good job and a good life. You have demoted me. This is the last time that I will listen to anything that you say." I blurted out in frustration. At first the Lord was silent as I complained. Finally, He decided to show me mercy and said, "Carry on complaining. When you really want my intervention you know what to do." So I apologised and changed my attitude.

The next day I was on the night shift which was to end at 9am the following day. All through the night, as I got ready to go to work, as I got on the bus and as I worked, I gave God thanks and praise because I was alive I was in my right mind to be able to work, I could now look forward to a salary at the end of the month and would not have to be a liability. I worked with a lot of enthusiasm and at 9am, although I was tired, as I walked from the restaurant to the bus stop I sang praises to God and just as I got on the bus my mobile phone rang. It was from a man named Dan (not real name) and he explained that he worked in a recruiting agency and had come across my CV. As he outlined the details, I realised that the CV he had seen was neither the doctored one nor the professionally written one but rather the badly written one. I cringed, *this is not going to be good* I thought and he confirmed it by pointing out the fact that I seemed to have done all my schooling in Nigeria.

"Yes", I answered, my voice a little above a whisper. *This is not good*, I thought again. Then he said that a company in the UK was looking to recruit a Document Controller who had worked in the Oil and Gas and that my CV showed I had this experience.

"Yes", I answered confidently starting to think, *this might not be so bad after all.* He asked if I was available for an interview the coming Monday and I said I was. He promised to send me the interview via email and true to his word, by the time I got home, a mail was waiting in my inbox with details for the interview. The organization in question was a global one and a visit to their website caused my heart to sink. Yes, I had worked in the Oil and Gas but not in a global organization. I shook my head and said to no one in particular, "They won't want to employ someone like me." Immediately the words left my mouth the Holy Spirit rebuked me sharply, "Do not say that!" Then He added, "When you go for your interview on Monday, make sure you arrive before time and ask to use their restroom. Take off your shoes and place your feet on the ground and declare that wheresoever the sole of your feet treads has been given to you for a possession."

As Monday approached, I realised I had a small challenge. My shift for the cleaning job on Sunday was a night one and I was due to finish the shift at 9am on Monday morning and my interview was for 11am. I knew there was no way I could arrive the interview on time if I went for the shift and if I did not go for the shift, since it was a new job and less than a week old, they would assume I was not serious and ask me not to turn up any longer and while that was okay if I got this new job, it would be a disaster if my interview was a flop and this global organization did not hire me. I shuddered to think what that would mean. I could not go through looking for a job again. So I went to the Lord in prayers. I said, "Lord this is the issue at hand, if I go to work I won't be able to make it for my interview. If I forgo the shift and my interview is a flop, once again I will be jobless. So what do I do? Do I go for the interview and forgo the shift and inevitably the cleaning job? I assumed the Lord was going to give me a clear direction, seeing I was very confused. I expected Him to say something like, "Thou shalt forgo the cleaning job and go for the interview because as thou goest for the interview the job shall be thine." Well He didn't, all He said to me was, "It depends on what you want." This answer was not what I was expecting and did nothing to help my confusion so I asked again. "Lord should I forgo the cleaning job and attend the interview?" Again He answered, "It depends on what you want." And He added, "If you want to be a cleaner go for your shift but if you don't want to be a cleaner then go for your interview." That settled it. I sent a text to the cleaning manager at the restaurant explaining that I was unable to make the Sunday shift for personal reasons and was happy to swop shifts with someone else if that was possible. She responded to say that it was not possible and I knew I had lost that job. I did not let that bother me. I would get paid for the three shifts I had already done.

Monday came and I went for my interview arriving early as directed by the Holy Spirit. The office manager came out to greet me and as I was ushered into a meeting room. I immediately asked to use the restroom and she gave me directions. Once inside, I took my shoes off and placed my feet on the ground. I reminded God of His word which says that where ever the soles of my feet shall tread will be given to me for a possession. I also reminded Him that His word says He will put the fear and dread of me upon all who are in the land to which I will come. I asked Him to give me the land for a possession and to place the fear and dread of me on everyone working in the organization, beginning with those who would interview me. I also asked Him to magnify me in the eyes of the interviewers so that I would appear bigger than I really am with regards to my qualifications and experiences.

When I returned the interviewers were not ready and as I waited alone in the meeting room my phone, which I had forgotten to turn off, began to ring. I answered it and it was another recruiting agency who wanted a Document Controller for a different company but this was a temporary position for one month. I told them I was available and they promised to call me again with an interview date. As I switched my phone off, the interviewers came into the room and the interview commenced. The interview lasted about forty five minutes, I tried to answer all the questions asked to the best of my ability all the time of course remembering that I was not alone but God was with me and magnifying everything I did and said, so even when I made a mistake it did not appear so. As the interview came to a close, I was informed that they had two applicants to interview for the same position the following day being Tuesday and after that they would give me a call to let me know how I fared. Then they wanted to know if I had any other plans as I would be required to resume the following week if taken. I told them about the other call that I received, explaining that the caller promised to call back with an interview date so I could not say what the rest of the week or the following week would bring. At this point they looked at each other and back at me and promised to get back to me after they had interviewed both people the following day. Later that day I got a call from the recruitment agent. He wanted to know if I was legally qualified to work in the UK and I said that I was. Then the following day the news I longed to hear came, the company had made me an offer and wanted to know if I would accept it. Accept it? Where they joking? I had accepted it even before I was interviewed. Then my employment letter and all the paperwork came in the post and I shared my testimony with my family who seemed very, very, surprised indeed. I resumed work on Tuesday the following week and the office manager said to me, of all the people we interviewed for this job, your CV spoke the loudest. I am thinking in my head. *My CV spoke the loudest? My 'badly written CV spoke the loudest? My CV that was not doctored to remove my Nigerian work experience spoke the loudest?* "Only you could have done it Lord" I muttered. She went on to say, "You were so confident during your interview; I bet you walked out of the meeting saying, yes, I have got the job." If only she knew how wrong she was. But I understood why she would think that. Remember, I had asked the Lord to magnify me? Well, that is exactly what He did.

Mediate on this: *"This day will I begin to put the dread of thee and the fear of thee upon the nations that are under the whole heaven, who shall hear report of thee, and shall tremble, and be in anguish because of thee."* Deuteronomy 2:25

Prayer: Father, I thank you because I enjoy your favour.

Eturuvie Erebor

DAY 17

12 Years Barrenness Ended

My name is Ogechi, I am from Delta State. I studied Catering and Hotel management at the famous ABU-Zaria. I was born thirty- five years ago in Kaduna State, with good education and looks I thought life would end up like one good bed time story, but I was wrong.

At the age of twenty-three I got married to Mr. Akinjide Teller, my first sweet heart that ended up being my worst mistake. In the first two years of our marriage I got pregnant twice but lost them after two months and three months respectively. At first, my husband who was a marketing executive showed great understanding and was ever supportive, but after I lost the third pregnancy everything changed. Akin or Akinzo as I and all members of my family fondly called my husband began to display some negative characteristics, he stopped taking his phone calls around me, he started returning home later than usual and forbade me from ever answering his phone calls. I noticed that a particular number called him the most, the name of the caller would show as Ella Recharge Card Girl. Initially, I did not take this as a serious issue because we were supposed to be good Christians. My husband started traveling and being away from town much longer than his usual two days' monthly routine check on the other branches of the company. Gradually, from two days out of town it increased to two weeks out of town, and then one month out of town.

When I tried to discuss my observations with him, we had the biggest family quarrel in the history of our marriage and for the first time called in his parents, who lived in the same town to settle us. To my surprise I was blamed, they said I was trying to hinder his career progress. Unknown to me, all of his actions had been orchestrated by his family and my offence was that after three years of marriage, I could not produce a child. Suspecting that something was very wrong, I diverted calls on his other phone to my phone and that was when I found out that I had been living with a familiar stranger, I called husband. I received a diverted call from this Ella, the so called recharge card girl. She assumed my husband had answered the call and asked him to please see her that day as she had done a double pregnancy test and was confirmed two months pregnant.

That day my husband returned home and told me that he was travelling for one week to south Africa for a marketing conference organized by an American pharmaceutical company for the introduction of an anti-retroviral drug which was intended to be presented to WHO (World Health Organization). I was happy for him so that night we prayed for God's guidance and blessings. The next morning my husband left for the airport. After one week he did not return and did not call, I waited another two days and when he did not return I went to his office and was told that my husband had since returned from the seminar, which I was told lasted three days. And he had been coming to the office. In confusion I left. I went to his father's house to inform his family but to my surprise I was not even allowed to enter the family house. Not knowing what to do I went to see my pastor and we began to pray to save my marriage. All attempt to reach him on phone failed, and his family members were no longer receiving my calls. News got to me that he was living with his ex-girlfriend who was at this time pregnant. I had lost a five-year-old marriage to barrenness. He lived in great affluence with his mistress and news about them, as the current celebrated couple was all over Lagos. I remained in our house praying, and asking God to restore my marriage. Then three months later I was sent a divorce letter. He confronted me face to face and told me to be reasonable and move on with my life because according to him his life was now better and more meaningful without me. I begged him and even sent friends and fellow Christians to him but he refused to have anything to do with me. He said that he was convinced by "his spirit" that I was a mistake. He said by revelation they (he and his family) saw that I was married in the marine world and was wasting his life and time. After all the attempts failed I signed the letter. Then one day I saw his driver who told me that my husband lost the baby he was expecting from his mistress and this was leading him to excessive drinking. Call me a fool if you like but I still cared for him so I sent mails to him consoling him and reminding him that God will give him a child.

Two years later, my over merciful land lord asked me to leave the house as I could not afford to renew the rent. I had nowhere to live so I was forced to go back to my parents' house. I only lived with my parents for a month before I saw the frustration that a failed marriage could bring. I lost all respect, I was mocked openly and was called a pregnancy sucking   witch.
Not being able to take it anymore, I left my parents' house and began to move from one friend's house to another. That also wasn't easy, but ONE DAY GOD STEPPED IN right on time when suicide was becoming sensible to me. After two years of being out of a five-year marriage I decided to bake a wedding cake for a friend even though I had stopped attending marriage celebrations because of shame and had begun to avoid touching children because I was convinced that I was cursed. When I agreed to bake my friend a wedding cake, I did not know that this cake would be the turning   point   in   my   story.
On the wedding day I was asked to talk about the cake, and when I finished a man walked up to me, and introduced himself as Engr. Paul Mokeme. He asked me if he could sit with me. I responded with a half-hearted, "Yes". He sat down and proceeded to tell me that he was a business man in town for some government business and he had been invited to the wedding by the Commissioner of Agriculture. We started talking, that conversation produced my second

husband whom I still happily married to. After I told him the story of my life he told me that with all his success he had not found the time to marry and if I agreed to let him be my first son he would marry me. I thought it was a joke but six weeks later we were married. Now, it is your time to shout hallelujah for me and every waiting/ expectant mother reading my story. After five years of being married to Paul we just had our first baby boy whom we named Emmanuel.

God's time does not follow human clock reading, I was married to my first husband for five years and begged and prayed and waited for him to return another two years and was married to my current husband whom I call my destiny for five years, totalling twelve years, before baby Emmanuel came. My question to you is how long have you waited? Hang in there and don't quit because God is doing something great in His miracle lab.

Meditate on this: *"And he said, I will certainly return unto thee according to the time of life; and, lo, Sarah thy wife shall have a son. And Sarah heard it in the tent door, which was behind him. Now Abraham and Sarah were old and well stricken in age; and it ceased to be with Sarah after the manner of women."* Genesis 18:10-11

Prayer: Lord give me the patience to wait on you knowing that you never fail.

Eturuvie Erebor

Day 18

Jesus.... I am Dead!

This happened many years ago. I was an undergraduate at the time. My school had just resumed after a six months' strike by the Academic Staff and I was really very excited because it meant, amongst other things, that I would get some money from my dad to do some shopping. And I love to shop. So I had gone out to do my shopping on the eve of resumption but on my way home I had seen a pair of shoes that I really liked but could not buy as I had used up all the money on me. Not a problem, I asked the shop attendant to hold it for me until close of business the following day as I would dash to the shop after my lectures to pay for them.

The following day, after my lectures, I was on my way to the shop. I stood at the bus stop waiting to catch a bus when all of a sudden the unexpected happened. A driver made a U-turn without any warning. This turn placed him on the fast lane of the traffic on the side of the road he had joined. So suddenly he was on the fast lane except that he wasn't going fast and it appeared he was struggling to get his car to accelerate. Another car was coming behind him and the driver was going really fast and as such was not prepared to stop suddenly and safely. In other to avoid running into the car that had suddenly entered the fast lane, he swerved his car. The intention was to join the other lane and overtake the driver who was still trying to come up to speed. However, he lost control of his car and instead of swerving into the other lane, he swerved off the road completely and made for the bus stop where I was standing. It all happened very quickly but as I watched the car approach, and at a speed I was knew the driver had no more control over, I was certain that it was the end for me. I saw my entire life flash before me and the last words I said, just before the car reached me, were "Jesus, I am dead!" I don't know what happened next but I saw myself in the air for less than a fraction of a second and then I was lying on the ground looking up at the sky and saying, "Jesus, I am not dead after all. I am alive. I am actually alive!" I tried to get up but someone asked me to lie still so I did. I was taken to the hospital to be examined and all I had was a sprained ankle. I could have lost my life and especially as I said with my own mouth that I was dead. And the Bible does say that life and death are in the power of the tongue and we shall have whatsoever we say. But God chose to show me mercy and preserve my life. Like I said, this happened many years ago but I still haven't been able to figure out how I walked away from that accident with only a sprained ankle. At a time, people ceased to believe that the car hit me. They thought I was only making it up since I didn't have an injury commensurate to the impact I described and what the other victims suffered. But I was there and I know that it did. And the impact should have been more on me as I was the first person the car made contact with. But God has given His angels charge over me to keep me in all my ways. Even when I am going out to buy a pair of shoes.

Meditate on this: *"For he shall give his angels charge over thee, to keep thee in all thy ways."* Psalm 91:11

Prayer: Father I thank you that you are concerned with my safety and that you have given your angels a charge over me to keep me in all my ways. I declare an angelic covering over my life and the lives of my loved ones in Jesus' name.

Eturuvie Erebor

Day 19

He Is Always On Time

When you are waiting on God to get married or for the blessing of the fruit of the womb, it can sometimes appear that He has forsaken you or that He does not care for you or feel your pains or understand your frustrations. And this feeing can be re-reinforced as you see other people getting married or having children. Suddenly you think, *yes I was right, He cares about others and doesn't care about me.* Yemi felt the same way after being childless for almost two decades. She was a child of God, she loved the Lord and had served Him faithfully for many years so she found it hard to understand why God would not give her children and especially when it began to be apparent that her husband and his family were becoming tired of the wait and seeking alternatives, alternatives which included wife number two to bear him children. She was heartbroken to say the least but she accepted it in good faith. What could she do? She was not the maker of children. She had asked children of the one who was the maker and who was also her father but had received none.

Right before her eyes arrangements were being made for the payment of the bride price of the second wife. She immersed herself in her job and kingdom activities so as to take her mind off what was happening in her marriage. Then as if she didn't have enough troubles, her health was challenged. Suddenly, she began to feel terrible excruciating pains in her abdomen which caused her to visit the doctor. Several tests were carried out and she was informed that she had fibroids which had to be removed. She returned home dejected. Now she had something else to worry about. At first she did not mention the diagnosis to her husband as she did not know how he would react. Lately he had been pulling away from her and was consumed with the excitement of marrying a woman who would bear him children. He seemed to spend his waking moments making plans for a future that did not include her. He had not asked her to leave, but she did not need to be told that their marriage was over and they were now two strangers living under the same roof. They no longer prayed together and he had moved out of their bedroom into another room which he would share with his new wife, when she moved in, following the payment of her bride price. However, he was still her husband and she had to tell him what was going on with her health and so she did. He advised that she agree with the doctors on a date to have the operation. Yemi did as she had been told and the day was fixed. When she informed him, he explained that he could not be at the hospital with her for the operation as it was the same day he was going with his family to be formally introduced to the family of his bride to be. Yemi was heartbroken but not surprised. She assured him that he didn't have to be there as her sister would be there with her. And so when the day finally arrived, Yemi left for the hospital to have her operation, while her husband left with his family to meet the family of the woman who would bear him children. As Yemi was taken into the theatre and up until the moment she lost consciousness, her only prayer was that God would preserve her life but God did not only hear and answer that prayer but He went ahead and answered the prayer that appeared to have gone unanswered for almost two decades.

Yemi went into the theatre to have fibroids removed. But when the doctors opened her up, there were no fibroids, but one…two…three baby boys. If you're wondering what happened to her hubby's plan to marry wife number two, your guess is as good as mine!

Meditate on this: *"There hath no temptation taken you but such as is common to man: but God is faithful, who will not suffer you to be tempted above that ye are able; but will with the temptation also make a way to escape, that ye may be able to bear it."* 1 Corinthians 10:13

"…For they shall not be ashamed that wait for me." Isaiah 49:23

Prayer: Father, I ask that you will give me the grace to wait on you for the blessings that you have for me. Help me to understand in the midst of the wait that you care for me and you will make everything beautiful in your time.

Eturuvie Erebor

DAY 20

A Second Chance

A young lady (let's call her Daniella) shared this testimony many years ago. And she shared it on the day that would have marked the 7th year anniversary of her death. This is what happened. Daniella was travelling with some friends from Abuja, the Federal Capital Territory of Nigeria, to Lagos. They planned to drive and this takes about 12 hours. As it would be a strain on one person, they decided to take it in turns driving the car. Everything was going well until they came to a town called Sagamu. By now they were about an hour and a half from their destination and everyone had had a turn behind the wheels. At Sagamu, they pulled off the road so they could change drivers for a final time. Daniella says that as soon as the young lady whose turn it was to drive, got behind the wheel, the Holy Spirit spoke to her and said, "Do not allow her drive." Daniella did not understand this request. They had planned their journey before they set out and it had been agreed that at Sagamu this lady would take over and drive them to Lagos. They were all responsible young adults and licensed to drive a car. What could be the problem? And also why would the Holy Spirit let everyone have a turn except this particular young lady? If she opened her mouth to say anything, she was certain it would lead to an argument and Daniella was not a confrontational person, so she remained silent and said nothing as the driver got behind the wheel and started the car. But Daniella had made a big mistake. One that would cost her, her life. Suddenly, the driver steered the car back into the busy express road without looking and narrowly escaped being crushed by a lorry which was on top speed and only a hair's breadth from their car. The lorry driver blared his horn which did nothing to help the nerves of the already frightened driver. Then of course her friends too began to scream all kinds of commands, "Stop the car," "Pull of the road," "Go faster", etc. In the midst of the confusion, she thought she was stepping on the breaks but she was really stepping on the accelerator and at the same time trying to do a zig zag to escape being hit by the lorry. She lost control of the vehicle which summersaulted and was rammed into by the lorry. Daniella was forcefully thrown out of the car, she hit the ground and instantly had an out of body experience. Suddenly, she was standing over her own body and she could see people running towards her. As they reached her, she heard them say, "She is dead. Let's help those who are alive." She watched helplessly as they put a cloth over her face and rush towards the car to help her friends out. They all seemed to be okay. They had cuts and bruises but they were fine. Then she turned to her own body which had been covered up and walked towards it. For some strange reason she can't explain, she was going back into her body and once she was fully inside her body, she felt a pain so intense that she cried out. Then people began to rush to her to help her. She was badly hurt and in a lot of pains and it would be months before she fully recovered, but she was alive. God had shown her mercy in spite of her disobedience to His warnings. He preserved her life. She had been given a second chance.

Meditate on this: *"For he saith to Moses, I will have mercy on whom I will have mercy, and I will have compassion on whom I will have compassion."* Romans 9:15

Prayer: Lord I thank you that you have chosen to show me your mercy. And I am grateful that your mercy overrides judgement.

Eturuvie Erebor

DAY 21

Help from Above

It was the year 1999. It was hmm, I think, the month of March. It was a Saturday morning and yes, it was me, behind the wheels of the metallic grey Honda Accord saloon. I was travelling from Benin to my hometown for the final stage of my grandfather's funeral rites. This stage involved the in-law's greeting. All the men who had married my grandfather's daughters were expected to be in attendance with members of their extended families to celebrate the life of the man who had been their father-in-law. It was usually a lavish ceremony as the in-laws used it to showcase their affluence and influence. I was really looking forward to it as I made my way out of Benin.

It was the first time I would drive outside Benin and I was excited and apprehensive at the same time. I had my younger sister with me in the front passenger seat and my aunt in the backseat. My sister did nothing to help my apprehension. As a matter of fact, she did everything to heighten it and there were moments I wished she was not in the car. I put some music on hoping that would calm her down. And it did but every now and then she would glance at the speedometer, look at me and then look away.

As we left Benin and hit the express road, my driving became steadier and everyone seemed to calm down and get absorbed in their own thoughts, thankfully. Then the unexpected happened. At first I wasn't sure what it was but I heard a loud bang and then it was almost as if I had lost control of the steering wheel. It no longer felt the same in my hand and I wasn't sure why. I stepped on my brakes gradually to reduce my speed but even that felt a little strange. Finally, the car came to a halt by the side of the road. Immediately, I looked at my sister and my aunt. They looked shaken but fine. I took off my seat belt, climbed out of the car and went around it to see what the issue was. Then I realised what had happened. The shaft had come off and damaged the tyre too.

"Oh my God!" I groaned.

"What is it?" My sister sounded every bit as alarmed as she looked, as she struggled to get out of the car.

As she saw what I had seen, her eyes widened.

"My goodness!" She exclaimed and looked at me. "What are we going to do?"

Before I could answer, our aunty had joined us.

"Hmm." She grunted. "We won't leave here today."

I rolled my eyes. *Did she have to be so negative?* I wondered.

I looked at the broken shaft and damaged tyre. My head was spinning as I wondered what the next line of action would be. We were in the middle of nowhere. There was no help in sight. Trying to stop a vehicle from there was pointless as no one would stop. People feared for their lives, and so when they travelled they did not stop on the road to help anyone for fear of being attacked and robbed or even killed. I sighed and ran one hand through my braided hair. This situation was a lot more serious than I realised when I first jumped out of the car.

"What do we do now?" My aunt asked me.

I did not reply but shook my head to indicate that I had no idea what to do. These were the days before mobile phones became available to all in Nigeria. Even if I decided to tow the vehicle back to Benin for repairs, I would still need to leave the breakdown spot to go into the nearest town to find a tow truck. And so far, leaving the spot was looking more and more impossible.

I sighed and looked up to heaven. I knew God answered prayers. He had answered me many times before and given me a miracle when I needed it most. I certainly needed one now. I said a silent prayer. I was a little confused and not sure what I really needed so I didn't get specific I just asked him to send me an angel to help me.

He heard and answered without delay because as soon as I was done praying in my heart, a Mercedes Benz 200 V-boot saloon pulled up in front of us. The car had gone past us on top speed, then it pulled off the road made a U-turn came to where we stood and stopped.

Three young men emerged from the car. They were three but at that instant my eyes saw only one man. He was the angel. He was tall, and yes, he was dark and handsome. He looked like he was Hausa and had on a white brocade kaftan with a matching cap. He walked towards me, his hand stretched out to shake mine.

"Hi." He greeted. "I am Danjuma (not real name). I am here to help."

I was so relieved to hear those words that I almost passed out. He noticed and smiled.

"As I drove by, I couldn't help but notice three women in distress standing by a broken down vehicle. You looked so helpless I had to come back. And I am glad I did."

He was God sent to us. He went into the nearest town and fetched a mechanic to fix the car. And he picked up the entire bill which included the cost of a new tyre, to replace the damaged one. And oh, lest I forget, he bought us lunch.

Meditate on this: *"The Lord hear thee in the day of trouble; the name of the God of Jacob defend thee; Send thee help* *from the sanctuary, and strengthen thee out of Zion."* Psalm 20:1-2

Prayer: Father, I ask that you will send me help, at every stage in my life, when I desperately need it.

Eturuvie Erebor

DAY 22

A Gentle Reminder Every Three Hours

My final exams as an undergraduate were over and I was preparing for one year of National Youth Service. As I waited for my call up letter, I began to pray about where I wanted to be posted for my service. I was aware that it was very possible for me to be posted very far from home and I did not want that. And then of course I also had in mind a place where I wanted to serve. I wanted to be posted to Abuja. As a matter of fact, many graduates wanted to be posted to Abuja for their service year. And why not? It is Nigeria's Federal Capital Territory and also the most beautiful city in the country. I had been to Abuja once but did not get a chance to see much of the city. What little I did see, I liked and I thought it wouldn't be a bad place to spend one year serving my country.

Unlike many others, my friends inclusive, who had the money and connections to ensure their posting to Abuja, I only had God. However, I believed that if I prayed, God would answer. So I began to pray every three hours. It was nothing big and complicated, just a gentle reminder, every three hours, that I wanted to be posted to Abuja.

Each time, I caught up with my friends they had some story about how they were making significant progress with regards to their posting. I began to wonder if perhaps, in addition to my prayers, I should ask them to help me and I did. But they explained that they could not help. Their connections could only help them out, no one else, unless of course they were willing to pay more. They could not afford to pay more, I could not afford to pay for myself, so I continued to pray and lobby God. At least I didn't have to give Him any money to arrange my posting to Abuja.

Finally, the day we had all been waiting for came. The postings had been published on the notice board in our school. I rushed into school, my heart beating really fast as I went. *What if God had not answered my prayer? What if instead of Abuja I had been sent up north to some dreaded place? How would I live there for an entire year?* The notice board was surrounded by final year students who were trying to find their names and posting. It took a while before I could get close to the board to actually see anything. There was a lot of noise; some people were rejoicing and others were bemoaning their predicament. And then there were those who were very bitter and very angry. No doubt those who took money from them to work their posting would have to refund it. As I looked for my name, I noticed that the state where each person was posted to was written next to their name, and the names before mine seemed to have very good postings so I hoped mine would be good even if it wasn't Abuja. Then I got to mine and next to my name was FC. Now that was not Abuja. But what was it? FC made no meaning to me. So in my confusion, I blurted out, "FC, where is that?" And some guy standing next to me gave me a playful slap on the shoulder and said excitedly, "FC stands for Federal Capital. Lucky girl, you've been posted to Abuja!" He was so excited you would have thought *he* was posted to Abuja. I was filled with such awe of God's faithfulness that I wasn't sure how to react. I was actually going to Abuja, for one year and I had done nothing to influence apart from a gentle reminder to God every three hours. Truly God answers prayers. What's more, my friends were not posted to Abuja.

Meditate on this: *"And he spake a parable unto them to this end, that men ought always to pray, and not to faint."* Luke 18:1

Prayer: Father, give me the grace not to quit before the answer comes.

Eturuvie Erebor

DAY 23

He is with Me Always

I was really excited about being posted to Abuja for my National Youth Service. The days leading up to my departure from home were spent putting together the things I required for trip. I had a few friends in Abuja and they had asked that I come to see them when I got into town and they would take me to the orientation camp. I was making the trip on a very tight budget so you can imagine what a disaster it was when I arrived at their house in Abuja and they were not there. It was the days before mobile phones existed in Nigeria so there was no way I could reach them. It was the final day for registration at camp so I had to be there unfailingly and the camp was on the outskirts of the city and it would cost an arm and two legs to get there by cab. Also because my friends had promised to help get me to camp I had no budget for my transport to camp. As I left their house in tears after waiting for more than three hours for their return, I was reminded of the Scripture that says, "Be not afraid nor dismayed, for the Lord your God is with thee wherever you go." (Paraphrased)

I walked on repeating those words to myself although I had no idea how it would help my present predicament. It was already getting dark, and it was drizzling, and there I was pulling my suitcase behind me in a town I was unfamiliar with and headed only God knew where. Suddenly, a car slowed down and pulled off the road next to me causing me to stop in my tracks. An elderly man was sitting in the back seat and he lowered his window to talk to me. He introduced himself as Dr William and wanted to know why I was crying. I thought that was strange because to begin with, his car had approached me from behind as I walked and since I had my back to him there was no way he would have known I was crying. Also it was getting dark and drizzling so he could not see the tear drops on my face. What was even more strange was that his voice and the expression on his face when he demanded to know why I was crying made me remember my late father. At that point he had looked and sounded like my dad. Anyway I didn't let myself dwell on that too much, without much ado I told him exactly why I was crying. Then he did something surprising. He asked me to get in so his driver could take me to camp. Before I could respond, he had ordered the driver to put my suitcase in the trunk of the car. Speechless, I got into the front seat next to the driver and we drove off. He explained that he had been on his way to his hotel to rest and added that if I didn't mind, the driver would drop him off and then take me to camp. And that was exactly what happened. The driver took him to the hotel and then took me to camp. I never saw or heard from Dr William again. His assignment in my life was over.

Meditate on this: *"Have not I commanded thee? Be strong and of a good courage; be not afraid, neither be thou dismayed: for the Lord thy God is with thee whithersoever thou goest."* Joshua 1:9

Prayer: Father, help me to remember that you are always with me to help me and to deliver me and as such I have no reason to fear or be discouraged.

Eturuvie Erebor

DAY 24

He Provides in Advance

After my one month stay at the orientation camp, I was faced with another challenge; accommodation. My late father had two friends in Abuja and I hoped one of them would accommodate me for the one year I was required to be in Abuja for my National Youth Service. They both seemed clearly reluctant to do this and I lived with one for about a month in which time he made it blatantly clear that I would be better off with the other friend. So I moved, but once I arrived at the other man's house it was the same story. He didn't want me to live with him. At this time, I was also having problems getting a place to do my primary assignment and as a result had stopped receiving the monthly allowance which the government paid to corps members serving the nation.

Well, obviously my problems were far from over so in the midst of that I also lost the roof over my head. I still remember the night my dad's friend had called me in for a chat and made it crystal clear that I had to leave. That night I could not sleep. I cried my eyes out as I had no idea what to do going forward and how to survive in a city where I knew very few people. And those few people had no desire to accommodate me. Well, the next morning I went to a business centre where I could make a few phone calls. I was trying to get a place so I could move out of my current accommodation. I was desperate and did not know what would happen if I returned home later that night to say I could not move out as I had no place to go. As I made my phone calls, things were not looking good and the tears began to well up in my eyes and then roll down my cheeks. It was a public place and I didn't want anyone to see me crying, so I reached into my handbag to get a handkerchief to wipe my eyes, and just then a business card fell out of my handbag. I bent to pick it up and immediately recollected that I had met the man in question the Sunday before. I was going to church and he had stopped and called me by some strange name I don't even remember what it was but I proceeded to tell him that I was not the person he thought I was. He had given me a ride to church and as he dropped me off, he handed me his business card and asked me not to hesitate to call him if I needed any assistance. As I looked at the card I couldn't help but wonder if this was the time to call him and if perhaps God had caused our paths to cross for such a time as this. I didn't wait for an answer, I just dialled his number. He sounded pleased to hear from me and when he asked if there was anything he could do for me, I just began to cry and speak at the same time. He knew it was serious so he asked where I was and told me to remain there as he was sending his driver to pick me. His driver picked me up and I didn't know where I was going but I had peace that it would be okay. He was at a friend's house and when I got there he introduced me and informed me that his friend had given me his hotel room in Agura Hotel for one week. This friend had come into the country from America to buy a house and upon his arrival, he had paid for a room in Agura Hotel for the duration of his stay. Well, with the house bought and renovated, he no longer required the room in Agura Hotel. It had been paid for but would expire in a week so it was really just a place for me to stay temporarily while I tried to work out a more permanent arrangement. I was relieved to say the least and thanked them profusely. Then the same driver was instructed to take me to pack my things and then to Agura Hotel.

Once again, God had shown up for me and used total strangers to provide for me. And knowing ahead what I required, He had provided it in advance.

Meditate on this: "…. *the Lamb slain from the foundation of the world.*" Revelation 13:8

Prayer: Father, Jesus is the Lamb slain from the foundation of the world. Before Adam and Eve sinned you had provided a remission for that sin. I thank you because you are providing for every need in my life even before they arise.

Eturuvie Erebor

DAY 25

He Provides in Advance (Part Two)

About two years ago I had to move house even though I wasn't ready for it financially and otherwise. The house I had lived in up on till that time had come fully furnished and I only had to move in with my suitcase. Now that I was forced to get another place I feared I may not be able to get the same deal and I did not have a budget for furnishing a house at the time. I went to view the house and just as I feared it was empty. I walked in and there was the landlord standing in the middle of the empty living room. He invited me to have a look around and when I was done I turned to him and said, "It's empty," as though that wasn't already obvious. He didn't answer, probably thinking it a rhetorical question. He just smiled and asked if I liked the place. *Yes, I liked the place but I could not afford to furnish it just yet!*

When I left, I prayed earnestly that he would not give me the place. He told me that a few people had come to view the house that same day so I was like, "Yeah. Please give it to one of them. I want to rent a furnished place." But I did not say this to his hearing. Well, a few minutes later I got a call saying the landlord was pleased to give me the place. Well, what could I do? I was desperate to find a place and I had found one, it was empty but it was better than being thrown out on the streets.

As I began to think about how I would furnish the place, especially as I was expecting my aunt in less than a week (she planned to visit for a month) I suddenly remembered that one of my brothers from church had visited me at home a few days prior to this time. During that visit, he had mentioned, in passing, a house where he was doing some renovation work as the owner wanted to sell it. The house was still fully furnished but the owner had asked him to get rid of the things and he had begun to give out the things. I immediately picked the phone and called him. He wanted to know what I would need and that was it. On the same day I moved into my empty house, my brother got a delivery truck to bring me the things I had asked for and on top of that, he paid for the delivery van.

Two days later, my aunty arrived for her holiday and she began to buy the items which I required but were missing. And so I got a fully furnished house without having to spend any money of my own.

Once again God proved that He always provides before the need arises. The problem is that many times we never ask the question, "Where is the provision?"

Meditate on this: *Consider the lilies how they grow: they toil not, they spin not; and yet I say unto you, that Solomon in all his glory was not arrayed like one of these.* Luke 12:27

Prayer: Lord I thank you because you care for me and are willing and able to meet all my needs and you do this always in advance. Open my eyes to see the provision for my current needs.

Eturuvie Erebor

DAY 26

Thanksgiving Brings Multiplication

God was sending me back to the UK. I had no idea what for but I had heard Him clearly. It wasn't exactly the most convenient time for me but I was willing to obey Him. I was a bit worried though because I had not been in the UK for a few years and I really didn't know what to expect. We talked about it (God and I) and agreed that I would travel over the Christmas holiday for two weeks just to see things for myself. This gave me less than two weeks to prepare and when I checked the prices of tickets my reaction was to completely ditch the idea. There was absolutely no way I was going to spend such a huge amount of money buying flight tickets for my daughter and I. But God had made other arrangements for me to buy my ticket without spending what I had in the bank.

A few days later, I got a call from a family friend (I had told her of my plan to relocate) and she said her husband would be coming into the town where I lived on business that weekend. She wanted me to go to see him as they had something for my daughter and I. According to her, it was a farewell gift from them. I thanked her and did as she said. Her husband came to my town on the weekend and I was able to see him. It was a very brief visit as he had a lot of people waiting to see him but I walked away from that meeting with enough money to buy our flight tickets. But what I found rather amazing is this; when he handed me the money, after counting it, I was certain that I heard him say, "This is two thousand dollars for you and your daughter." This was great because it was a gift, I was not expecting it and I was grateful. However, I would still have to add to it to buy our tickets. Now, here is where it gets interesting. When I got home, inspired by Luke 9:16, I lifted up the money and gave God thanks for it. When I was done, the Holy Spirit clearly said to me, "Count the money". Prior to this time, I had not done so. I obeyed and counted the money. It was three thousand dollars. This meant I would not have to use my money to purchase the ticket. God had provided for it just as He said He would. Now, I don't know if and when the money changed from two thousand dollars to three thousand dollars. Perhaps, I heard wrong. Perhaps God increased it as I prayed. I will never know. What I do know though, is that three thousand dollars was what I required, if I wasn't going to put some of my money towards the purchase of the tickets. And three thousand dollars was what God gave to me.

When we give thanks for what is not enough, God multiplies it so that it becomes more than enough.

Meditate on this: *"Then he took the five loaves and the two fishes, and looking up to heaven, he blessed them, and brake, and gave to the disciples to set before the multitude. And they did eat, and were all filled: and there was taken up of fragments that remained to them twelve baskets."* Luke 9:16

Prayer: Father, I lift up everything in my life that is not enough and I thank you for providing them in the first instance.

Eturuvie Erebor

DAY 27

Thanksgiving Brings Multiplication (Part Two)

After paying my tithe and purchasing the flight tickets for my daughter and I, there was nothing left from the money God had miraculously provided for our trip. This meant that I would have to take our travel pocket money from my account. I worked out how much I was comfortable removing from the account without messing up my other plans. We had to go in to Lagos to catch our flight and prior to that time I had been getting promptings from the Lord to buy my travel money but I kept putting it off. I wanted to do it in Lagos and I knew the exact place, my mind was made up to buy my travel money there. Well, I can tell you now that it was not a good move. I should have listened to the Lord because He sees what I don't see and He knows what I don't know. But on this occasion I did not listen to Him and I paid dearly for it. I was defrauded and lost a good amount of my travel money. There was little or no time to do anything about it as I had a plane to catch.

As I made my way to the airport, I was not a very happy person but I decided to give God thanks all the same. I thanked Him because He had actually warned me although I did not listen. I thanked Him because I realised I could have lost more than I had already lost. I thanked also because by now I understood that when what you have is not enough, thanking God for it, causes it to multiply. I did not know how the money in my hand would multiply though, but I thanked Him all the same.

When we arrived in London, a cousin of mine came to visit us. She had quite a lot of letters for me as she had been receiving my letters while I was away in Nigeria. As I began to go through the letters, I came across one from my bank, I opened it and realised that it was my bank statement. Now, before I left the country I had removed everything in my bank account as I needed the money and so I was not expecting to see any money in my account. However, there was a payment I had been expecting from the government prior to leaving the country five years earlier but the money never came before I left and I had forgotten about it completely. Well that money did come after I left the country and it was now sitting in my account as a tidy one thousand one hundred pounds. Not a bad amount for unexpected travel money, I am sure you will agree.

Once again, God proved in my life that when we thank Him for whatever is not enough, He multiplies it so that it becomes more than enough.

Meditate on this: *"And he took the seven loaves and the fishes, and gave thanks, and brake them, and gave to his disciples, and the disciples to the multitude. And they did all eat, and were filled: and they took up of the broken meat that was left seven baskets full."* Matthew 15:36-37

Prayer: Father, I thank you because you are able to meet all of my needs and you are able to transform lack to abundance. I decree that every lack in my life is now turned into abundance. I enjoy an abundance of every good thing, in Jesus' name.

Eturuvie Erebor

DAY 28

He Will Make a Way

When my daughter and I arrived at the airport, I was still disheartened over my lost travel money but I was determined to keep thanking God and praising Him until my mood changed. God was bigger than the challenge. He had provided for me many times and He had restored what I thought was lost so I could trust Him. Little did I know at the time that some stolen travel money was the very least of my problems. As we arrived the British Airways desk at the departure hall, the lady took the British Passports of my daughter and I looked through them and announced, "Madam, your baby's passport has expired."

My heart skipped a beat and I gave her a blank stare, like, what are you on about?

"No, it hasn't expired." I said and collected the passport from her to have a look for myself.

Well, it turns out that she was right; my daughter's passport had expired. Now my heart really sank but I remained calm.

She advised me to go to the British High Commission and have it renewed. The implication of that was that we could not travel that night. It also meant we would have to spend the weekend in Lagos to be able to be at the High Commission on Monday. If they attended to us, then perhaps we could travel the same night or….

The more I thought about it, the more it was turning out to be a real nightmare. Oh, how could I have been so careless? I just assumed that because my passport was valid for ten years, my daughter's was also valid for ten years. Hence, I never really looked or I would have seen that it was valid for five years and had expired in August of that same year.

Suddenly I was exhausted. It had been a long day, I had been defrauded and now it looked like I may lose the money for our tickets because I was already resolved not to travel. I would go upstairs to the British Airways office and explain the situation, all I had to lose was the ticket money, life would go on. As I got to the office, I took a ticket and sat down, waiting to be called. While waiting I entered into a conversation with God.

"Why did you give me three thousand dollars?" I asked

"So you could buy your ticket and make this trip." Was His response.

"Good." I responded. "As it stands, we can't make this trip and we may lose the money for the ticket as I do not even know what the refund policy is and right now I am exhausted and I have decided I won't make this trip."

The Lord did not answer me. He did not have to. Just as I finished talking and blurting out my frustrations, the lady who had spoken to me downstairs rushed into the room and said. "I just spoke to a senior colleague of mine. British Airways will carry you even with the expired passport, we just need to check to ensure it is not fake."

So I went downstairs with her and she took the passport from me and handed it to her colleague who disappeared with it for about ten minutes. When he returned he smiled and said, "You may now check in, Madam."

Once again God showed up for me and proved that when He asks you to go somewhere nobody can cause you to return. All you have to do is trust Him. He will always make a way.

Meditate on this: *"Behold, I will do a new thing; now it shall spring forth; shall ye not know it? I will even make a way in the wilderness, and rivers in the desert."* Isaiah 43:19

Prayer: Father, please give me a way of escape out of every situation that seeks to weary me and cause me to quit.

Eturuvie Erebor

DAY 29

God is Enough

Many years ago, a cousin of mine was having challenges gaining admission into university. Although he had done well on his GCE, he had not done too well on his JAMB. He did not fail, but he did not meet the cut off for the course of his first choice. The way forward was for him to be offered a place in the course of his second choice as he clearly met and surpassed the cut off mark for this course. But sadly, for this to happen, we would have to give someone a bribe.

Many people began to suggest all kinds of things but I was at a point in my life where I was beginning to experience God in a way that I had never experienced Him before and so I said to my cousin, "You don't need any man. You only need God, God is enough." At first he looked at me with some doubt but as I shared testimonies of God's faithfulness in my life, he finally agreed to let God have His way. He went with me to church and gave his life to Christ and I promised him that God was going to give him a testimony that he would remember for a long time to come. I did not know what the testimony was but I was certain it would be something that would make him trust God even more with every segment of his life.

Well, one day after church, a friend of his came to visit him at home and the friend was so excited that from the moment he set eyes on my cousin the first thing he said was, Congratulations on your admission." My cousin was both surprised and confused and wanted to know why he was being congratulated. As far as he was concerned, he had not been given any admission as he had taken my advice and didn't bribe anyone. He had even decided at that point to re-write his JAMB exams. His friend was a taken aback by his question and said, "Your admission into Uniben."

Now my cousin thought his friend must be losing it. He responded, "Admission? What admission are you talking about?" There was a bit of back and forth and then we got to the bottom of the matter. My cousin's friend had gone to the school's notice board the day before to look for a friend's name. As he looked through the list, he had seen my cousin's name on the board. He thought my cousin already knew but did not realise that in coming to congratulate him, he was actually informing him. Now my cousin had chosen to study Computer Science but he didn't make the cut off and we refused to bribe anyone, choosing to hold on to God. Well, God sorted it all out by Himself. Mysteriously, my cousin was offered a place in Mathematics. My cousin has long graduated and we still don't know how his name got on the list. But I know God did it. He confirmed what I had told my cousin, that He is more than enough.

Meditate on this: *But Jesus beheld them, and said unto them, With men this is impossible; but with God all things are possible.* Matthew 19:26

Prayer: Father I thank you because with you all things are possible.

DAY 30

Whatever He Does is Forever

Years ago, while living in Nigeria and working with a very large indigenous organization, I faced a lot of challenges which caused me to quit my job without talking to God about it. I wrote my resignation, handed it in, cleared my desk and went home. I had had enough. Well, I had, but apparently God hadn't, so when I got home He began to speak to me.

He wanted me to go back to the organization as it was not yet time for me to leave. He told me that they would send for me and I would get a pay rise. He added that when I got the pay rise, I was to return to work and keep my mouth shut about all other grievances that I had. I agreed and the following day I got a phone call. The company's Managing Director wanted to see me. So I went to see him. He went straight to the point; I was a good staff and the organization was happy to look at my grievances and resolve them. As the Lord had told me I would get a pay rise, I brought this up and a negotiation ensued. When we had reached an agreement, HR was called in to issue me a letter advising me of my move to new department (which was in itself a promotion) plus my pay rise. The following week I resumed work in my new department and tongues were wagging everywhere. Many called me the MD's pet, others called me his favourite. Well, it didn't take long before all of their talk got to the attention of the Group Managing Director who immediately asked the MD to report to headquarters. When the MD returned from his trip the following day, he sent for me. He was not happy and informed me of all that had transpired. The GMD had insisted that my pay rise be revoked immediately and an email had been sent to the company's account department to disregard the letter I had received from HR and continue to pay me my old salary. I remained calm because I knew what God had told me. I thanked him for his effort in providing me a pleasant employment experience and went on to tell him that contrary to what he thought, he had not given me a pay rise, God had. I asked to have the day off and I left. I wanted to be in church (although there was no service but I know God is always in Zion).

On my way, God came to me and whispered, "Who says a thing and it comes to pass when the Lord has not commanded it?" As that was sinking it, He added, "Whatsoever the Lord doeth, it shall be forever, nothing can be added to it and nothing taken from it." And finally, He assured me that the organization did not belong to the GMD even though the GMD thought it did. Ultimately, it belonged to Him (God) my father, because the earth is the Lord's and the fullness thereof, the world and all they that dwell therein. On that note He asked me to send a message to the GMD stating that because I was a daughter of God he could not demote me. I sent the message as God instructed. I never got a response from him, not that I expected one. At the end of the month, when salaries were paid, I was not paid my old salary but my new salary. And for the next eighteen months, until God said it was time to leave, no one could touch the pay rise God had given to me. Truly, He owns it all and when He gives a blessing, no one can reverse it.

Meditate on this: *"Who is he that saith, and it cometh to pass, when the Lord commandeth it not?"* Lamentations 3:37

"The earth is the Lord's, and the fulness thereof; the world, and they that dwell therein." Psalm 24:1

Prayer: Father, I magnify you above every situation in my life. You are God and you hold the whole world in your hands, and determine the occurrences, therefore I refuse to be afraid.

Eturuvie Erebor

56375007R00067

Made in the USA
Lexington, KY
20 October 2016